A-Z ST. ALBANS

C000252384

CONT...

REFERENCE

Motorway	M1	**Car Park** Selected	P
A Road	A414	**Church or Chapel**	†
B Road	B653	**Fire Station**	■
Dual Carriageway		**Hospital**	H
One-way Street Traffic flow on A Roads is indicated by a heavy line on the driver's left.	➡	**House Numbers** A & B Roads only	22 11
		Information Centre	i
Restricted Access		**National Grid Reference**	520
Residential Walkway	·········	**Police Station**	▲
Track	=========	**Post Office**	★
Footpath	---------	**Toilet**	▽
Local Authority Boundary	— · — · —	with facilities for the Disabled	♿
Postcode Boundary	— — — —	**Educational Establishment**	
Railway	Station ⇄	**Hospital or Hospice**	
		Industrial Building	
Built-up Area	WEST AV	**Leisure or Recreational Facility**	
		Place of Interest	
Map Continuation	10	**Public Building**	
		Shopping Centre or Market	
		Other Selected Buildings	

Scale

1:15,840

0 — ¼ — ½ Mile

0 — 250 — 500 — 750 Metres

4 inches (10.16 cm) to 1 mile
6.31cm to 1km

Geographers' A-Z Map Company Ltd.

Head Office:
Fairfield Road, Borough Green, Sevenoaks, Kent, TN15 8PP
Telephone 01732 781000 (General Enquiries & Trade Sales)

Showrooms:
44 Gray's Inn Road, London, WC1X 8HX
Telephone 020 7440 9500 (Retail Sales)
www.a-zmaps.co.uk

Ordnance Survey®

This product includes mapping data licensed from Ordnance Survey® with the permission of the Controller of Her Majesty's Stationery Office.

© Crown Copyright 2001. Licence Number 100017302

Edition 2 2001

Copyright © Geographers' A-Z Map Co. Ltd. 2001

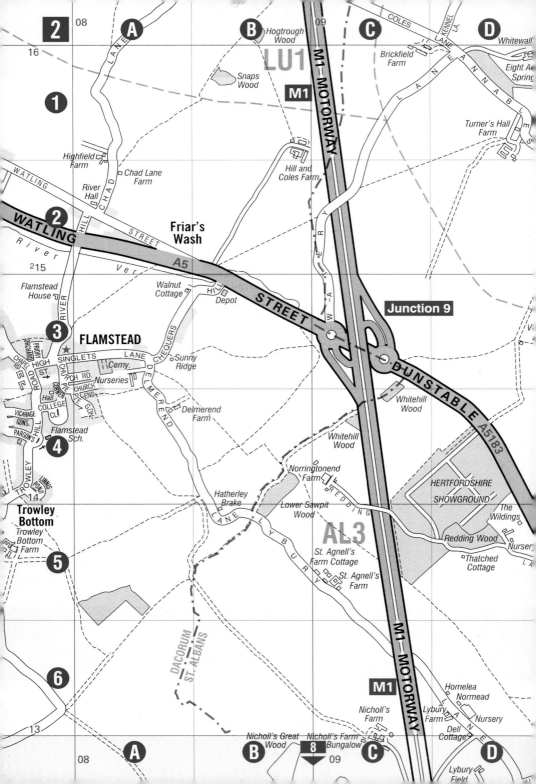

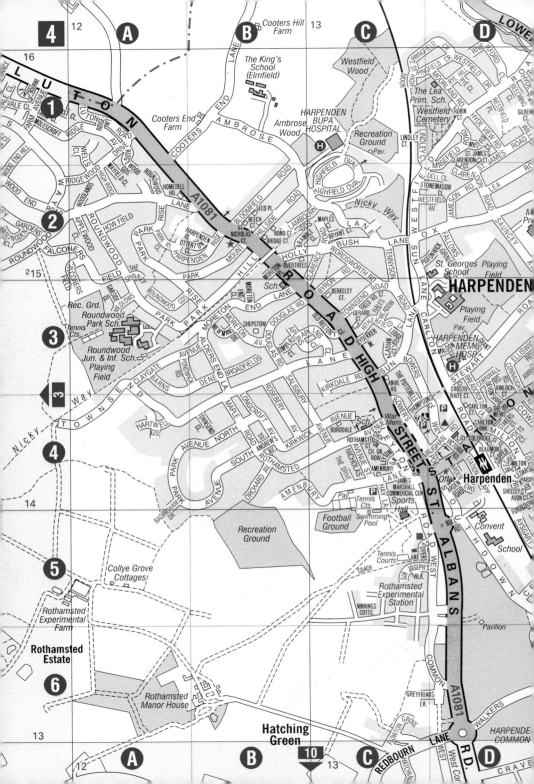

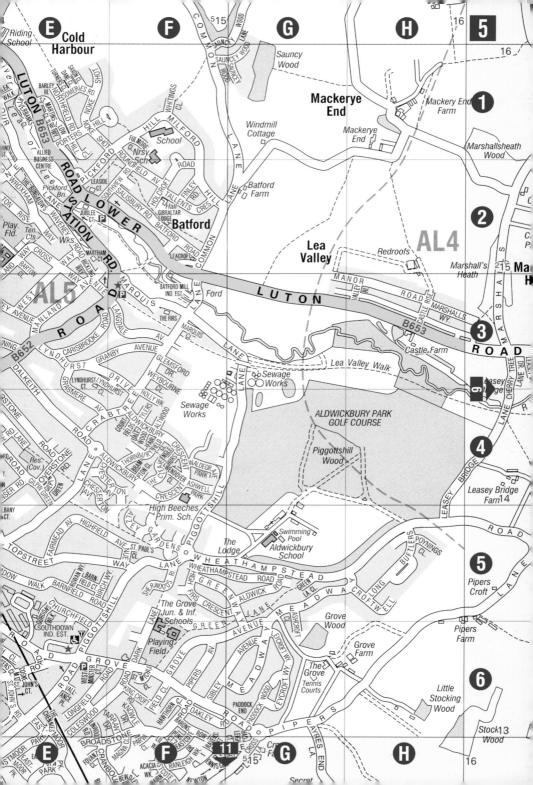

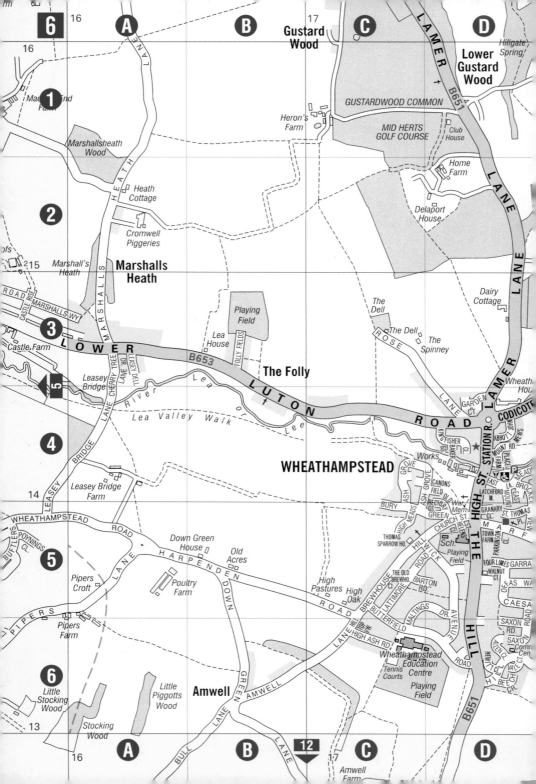

LAMER PARK

Round Spring

Bride Hall

WELWYN HATFIELD
ST. ALBANS

HILL FARM LANE

1

Stocking Springs

Little Norfolk Wood

Great Norfolk Wood

Lamerwood Country Club

AL6

R O A D

2

Scratching Grove

Threegroves Wood

2 15

Lamer Farm

Cherrytree Spring

3

D D I C O T E

L A N E

S H E E P C O T E

CORY-WRIGHT

Black Bridge

Robinson's Wood

4

The Watersplash

Lea valley Walk

Lea or Lee

Sewage Works

ports ound

AL4

River

L A N E

B653

Marford Farm

14

Gray's Wood

NECTON RD

W A Y

SHEEPCOTE

R O A D

The White Cottage

5

TUDOR RD

MARFORD

B653

Charlies Croft

BATTLE-VIEW

LAMB CT.

ROAD

L A N E

B E E C H H Y D E

L A N E

W A T E R E N D L A N E

R O A D

Devil's Dyke

David's Dingle

6

SMALL WD CL

DAVYS CL.

ES RD

Chalkdell Farm

The Slad

B E E C H H Y D E L A

Samuels Farm

G R E E N L A N E

Beech Hyde Farm

Belgic Oppidum

13

A

B

C

D

Manor House

Hatching Green
4

LA.
VERS
HARPENDEN
COMMON

CRAVELLS

1
R E D B O U R N
B487

Deacon's Spring

Harpenden Rugby Club

POWTON GROVE

HATCHING GREEN CL.

HIGH ELMS

HIGH ELMS

THE WARREN

WEST COMMON

WEST COMMON

ST ALBANS A1081

HARPENDEN COMMON

LIMBRICK

Lim
H

ROAD

HA.
CO
GOLF

OAKHURST AV.

OAKFIELD ROAD

DELLCROFT WAY

WEST COMMON CL.

WEST COMMON

WEST COMMON GROVE

ROAD

CRO

2
12

HARPENDEN GOLF COURSE

Hammondsend Farm

HAMMONDS END LANE

Club House

FAIRWAY CL.

OAKFIELD ROAD WEST

OAKVIEW CL.

OAKWOOD DRF.

GARDEN CL.

WEST

UPLANDS

THE

BARLINGS RD.

BARLINGS

COLLENS RD.

THE CHOWNS

BURYWICK

BURYWICK

MAPLE COTTS.

BURY-WICK

BEESONEND

3

Hammondsend Wood

HAMMONDS

HAMM

THE PROSPECT

OAK WAY

OAKFIELD

WHEATFIELD RD.

WHEAT

PENNY CROFT

THE LANE

DEERINGS

HANSLEY ROAD

NETHERFIELD

NR. POP. E

BEESONEND COTTAGES

AL5

9

4

Beesonend Farm

Stud Wood

Childwick Stud

Childw
Hall

11

Walk

ournbury
Mill

Ford

5
Redbournbury

REDBOURNBURY LANE

MILL

BEESONEND

Hedge's Farm

STUD SCHOOL

Mannings Cottage

Bush Wood Cottages

6

Stream

Works

Bush Wood

210

River Ver

Mill Race

New Jerome

The

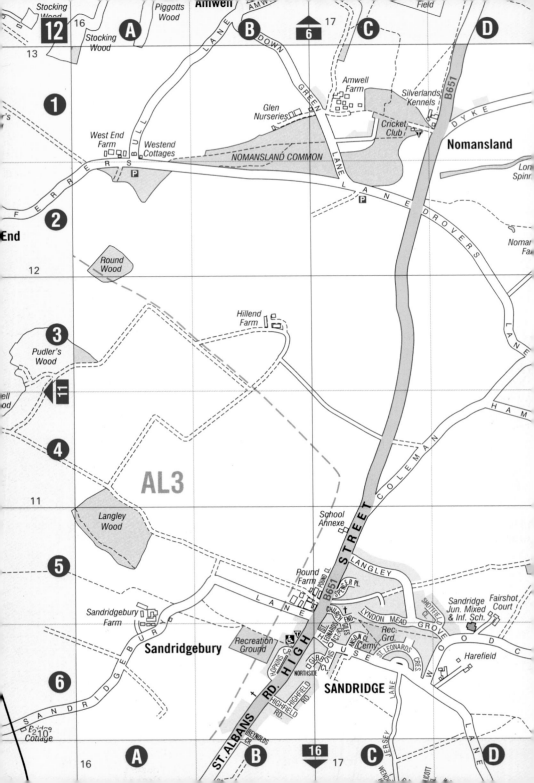

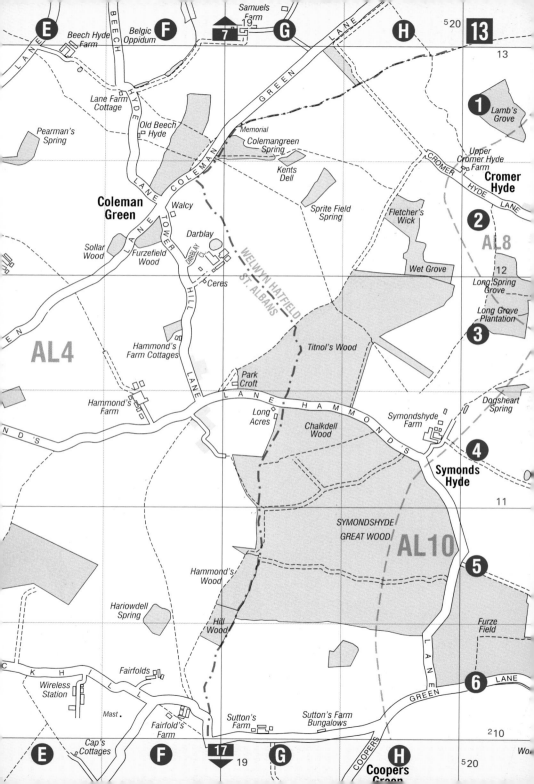

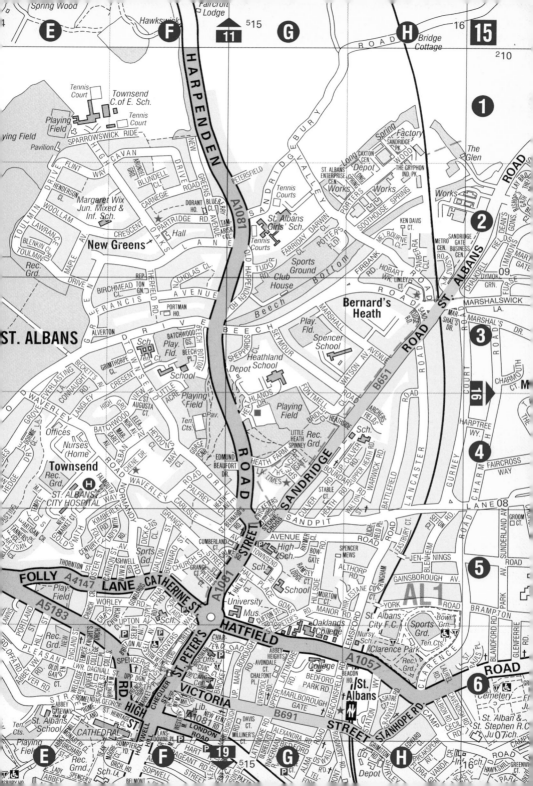

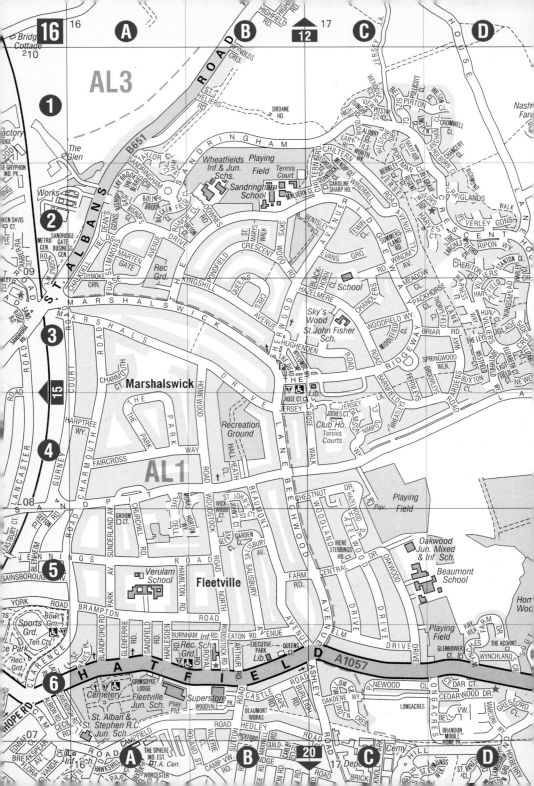

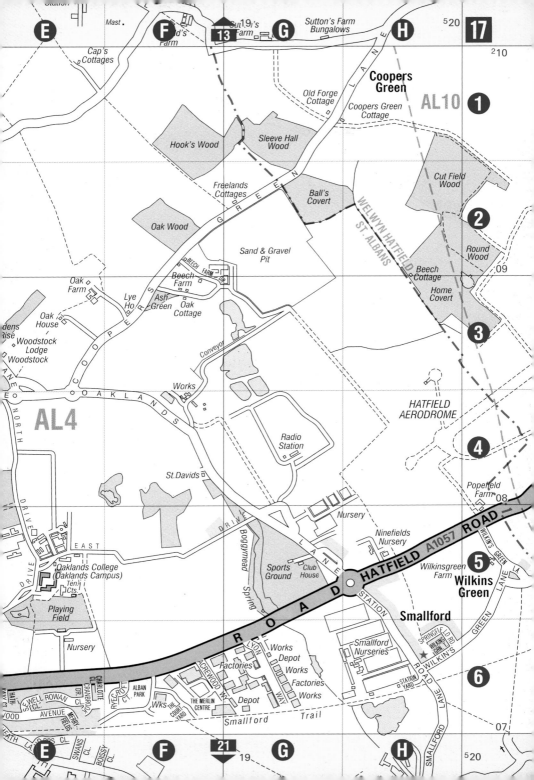

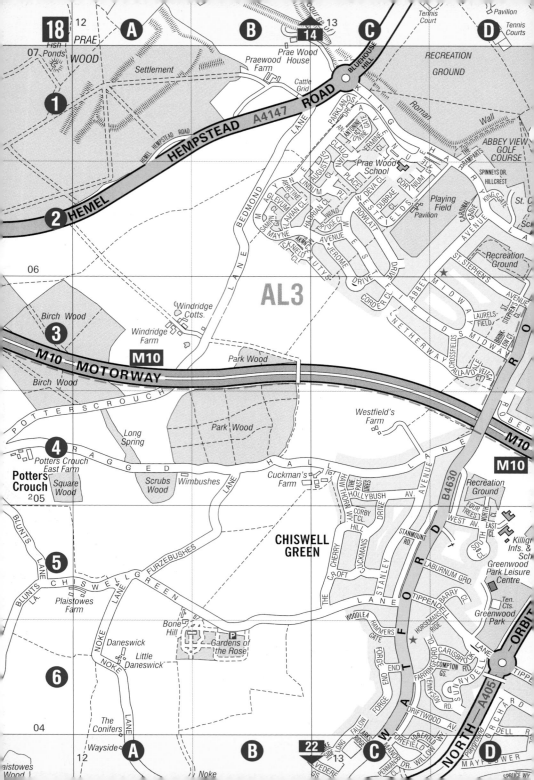

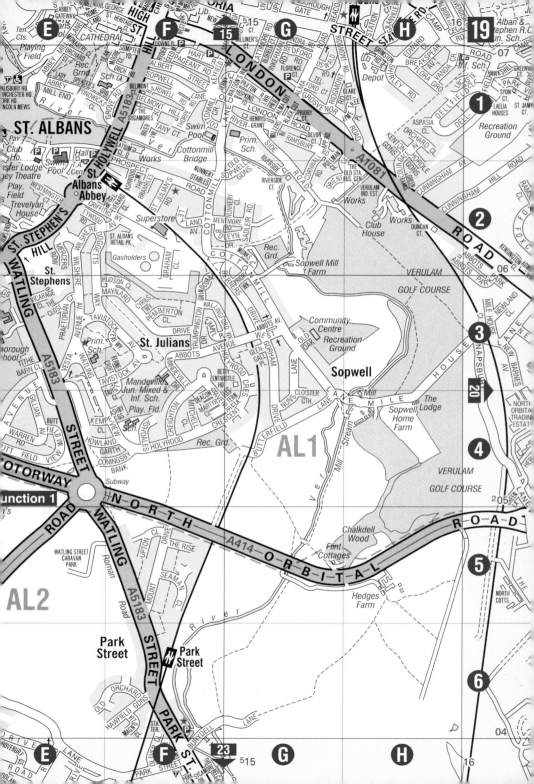

A **B** **C** **D**

20

QUARRY

1

Conolly House

DRIVE

Napsbury

Pavilion

Ten. Cts.

Playing Field

Piggery

2

M25 MOTORWAY

M25

3

Warehouses

23

Springfield Farm

Colne

4

Old Parkbury

Works

River

5

Miniature Railway

B556

Lodge

Radlett Golf Cen.

Houndswood Farm

Houndswood

Hound's Wood

6

Harper Lodge Farm

Harper House

WATLING STREET

HARPER

SHENLEY

B5378

ST. ANNES

MANOR FORD

COLLYER RD.

WALSINGHAM WY.

SUMMERFIELD CL.

Bowmansgreen Prim. Sch.

Lib.

Prim. Sch.

BLUETT RD.

SANDERS CL.

BIRCH RD.

THE GRN.

ST. ANNE'S

HARDWICKE CT.

HEATHER CT.

South Farm Cottages

South Lodge

Barley-Mo-Farm

Fir Tree Farm

Broad Colney Bridge

WATER

Depot

AL2

Farm

Pastoral Centre (Convent)

Broad Coln

LANE

LANE

The Cottage

Colney Park

Electricity Sub. Station

Nursery

Sports Pav. Ground

Bowl. Grn.

Ten. Cts.

Swim. Pool

H

Radlett Lodge Sch.

HARPERBURY HOSPITAL

HERTSMERE

ST. ALBANS

Playground

Nine Acres

Model Farm

Wild Farm

Monks Wood

WAYSIDE

04

203

02

01 16

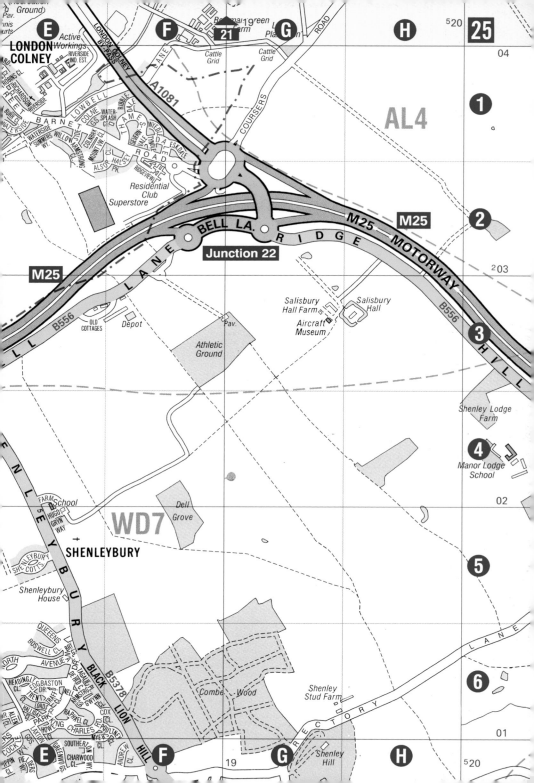

INDEX

Including Streets, Places & Areas, Industrial Estates,
Selected Subsidiary Addresses, and Selected Places of Interest.

HOW TO USE THIS INDEX

1. Each street name is followed by its Posttown or Postal Locality and then by its map reference; e.g. Ambrose La. *Hpdn* —1B **4** is in the Harpenden Posttown and is to be found in square 1B on page **4**. The page number being shown in bold type. A strict alphabetical order is followed in which Av., Rd., St., etc. (though abbreviated) are read in full and as part of the street name; e.g. Apple Tree Gro. appears after Applecroft but before Applewood Clo.

2. Streets and a selection of Subsidiary names not shown on the Maps, appear in the index in *Italics* with the thoroughfare to which it is connected shown in brackets; e.g. *Alban Ct. St Alb —6B 16 (off Burleigh Rd.)*

3. Places and areas are shown in the index in **bold type**, the map reference to the actual map square in which the Town or Area is located and not to the place name; e.g. **Amwell. —6B 6**

4. An example of a selected place of interest is **Abbey View Golf Course. —1D 18**

GENERAL ABBREVIATIONS

All : Alley
App : Approach
Arc : Arcade
Av : Avenue
Bk : Back
Boulevd : Boulevard
Bri : Bridge
B'way : Broadway
Bldgs : Buildings
Bus : Business
Cvn : Caravan
Cen : Centre
Chu : Church
Chyd : Churchyard
Circ : Circle
Cir : Circus
Clo : Close
Comn : Common
Cotts : Cottages

Ct : Court
Cres : Crescent
Cft : Croft
Dri : Drive
E : East
Embkmt : Embankment
Est : Estate
Fld : Field
Gdns : Gardens
Gth : Garth
Ga : Gate
Gt : Great
Grn : Green
Gro : Grove
Ho : House
Ind : Industrial
Info : Information
Junct : Junction
La : Lane

Lit : Little
Lwr : Lower
Mc : Mac
Mnr : Manor
Mans : Mansions
Mkt : Market
Mdw : Meadow
M : Mews
Mt : Mount
Mus : Museum
N : North
Pal : Palace
Pde : Parade
Pk : Park
Pas : Passage
Pl : Place
Quad : Quadrant
Res : Residential
Ri : Rise

Rd : Road
Shop : Shopping
S : South
Sq : Square
Sta : Station
St : Street
Ter : Terrace
Trad : Trading
Up : Upper
Va : Vale
Vw : View
Vs : Villas
Vis : Visitors
Wlk : Walk
W : West
Yd : Yard

POSTTOWN AND POSTAL LOCALITY ABBREVIATIONS

A'ham : Aldenham
Ay L : Ayot St Lawrence
Brick : Brickendon
Brick W : Bricket Wood
Childw : Childwickbury
Col H : Colney Heath
Col S : Colney Street
E Hyde : East Hyde

Els : Elstree
Flam : Flamstead
Frog : Frogmore
Hpdn : Harpenden
Hem H : Hemel Hempstead
Lem : Lemsford
Lon C : London Colney
Mark : Markyate

Naps : Napsbury
Oakl : Oaklands
Park : Park Street
Pep : Pepperstock
Port W : Porters Wood
Rad : Radlett
Redb : Redbourn
St Alb : St Albans

Sandr : Sandridge
Shenl : Shenley
Smal : Smallford
Tyngr : Tyttenhanger
Wat : Watford
Welw : Welwyn
Wheat : Wheathampstead

INDEX

Abbey Av. *St Alb* —3C **18**
Abbey Gateway. *St Alb* —6E **15**
Abbey Mill End. *St Alb* —1E **19**
Abbey Mill La. *St Alb* —1E **19**
Abbey Vw. *St Alb* —2F **19**
Abbey View Golf Course.
    —1D **18**
Abbey Vw. Rd. *St Alb* —6E **15**
Abbots Av. *St Alb* —3G **19**
Abbots Av. W. *St Alb* —3F **19**
Abbots Pk. *St Alb* —2A **20**
Abbott John M. *Wheat* —4D **6**
Acacia Wlk. *Hpdn* —1F **11**
Acadian Ct. *Hpdn* —3C **4**
Acers. *Park* —2E **23**
Acorns, The. *St Alb* —6D **16**
Acrewood Way. *St Alb* —6F **17**
Adelaide St. *St Alb* —5F **15**
Admirals Wlk. *St Alb* —2A **20**
Akeman Clo. *St Alb* —2B **18**
Alban Av. *St Alb* —4F **15**
Alban Ct. St Alb —6B 16
   (off Burleigh Rd.)
Alban Pk. *St Alb* —6F **17**
Albany Ct. *Hpdn* —5E **5**
Albany Ga. St Alb —1F 19
   (off Belmont Hill)
Albany M. St Alb —1C 22
   (off N. Orbital Rd.)

Albert St. *St Alb* —1F **19**
Albion Rd. *St Alb* —6H **15**
Aldbury Clo. *St Alb* —1C **16**
Alder Clo. *Park* —2D **22**
Alders End La. *Hpdn* —3B **4**
Aldwick. *St Alb* —2B **20**
Aldwickbury Cres. *Hpdn* —4F **5**
Aldwick Ct. *St Alb* —2B **20**
Aldwick Rd. *Hpdn* —5G **5**
Alexander Rd. *Lon C* —5C **20**
Alexandra Rd. *St Alb* —6G **15**
   (in two parts)
Allandale. *St Alb* —3D **18**
Allen Clo. *Shenl* —6E **25**
Allen Clo. *Wheat* —6D **6**
Allied Bus. Cen. *Hpdn* —1E **5**
Alma Cut. *St Alb* —1G **19**
Alma Rd. *St Alb* —1G **19**
Almonds, The. *St Alb* —4B **20**
Alsop Clo. *Lon C* —2E **25**
Althorp Rd. *St Alb* —5H **15**
Altwood. *Hpdn* —4F **5**
Alverton. *St Alb* —3E **15**
Alzey Gdns. *Hpdn* —5F **5**
Amberley Clo. *Hpdn* —3D **4**
Ambleside. Hpdn —3F 5
   (off Langdale Av.)
Ambrose La. *Hpdn* —1B **4**
Amenbury Ct. *Hpdn* —4C **4**

Amenbury La. *Hpdn* —4B **4**
Amwell. —6B 6
Amwell La. *Wheat* —6B **6**
Anderson Ho. *St Alb* —1D **20**
Andrew Clo. *Shenl* —6F **25**
Annables La. *Hpdn* —1D **2**
Anson Clo. *St Alb* —2B **20**
Anson Clo. *Sandr* —6C **12**
Antonine Ct. *St Alb* —1C **18**
Antonine Ga. *St Alb* —1C **18**
Anvil Ho. *Hpdn* —3C **4**
Aplins Clo. *Hpdn* —3B **4**
Applecroft. *Park* —2D **22**
Apple Tree Gro. *Redb* —1F **9**
Applewood Clo. *Hpdn* —2A **4**
Approach Rd. *St Alb* —1G **19**
Aran Clo. *Hpdn* —1F **11**
Archers Clo. *Redb* —2F **9**
Archers Fields. *St Alb* —4H **15**
Arden Gro. *Hpdn* —4D **4**
Ardens Way. *St Alb* —3D **16**
Ardentinny. St Alb —1G 19
   (off Grosvenor Rd.)
Armstrong Clo. *Lon C* —1E **25**
Armstrong Gdns. *Shenl* —6E **25**
Arretine Clo. *St Alb* —2B **18**
Arthur Rd. *St Alb* —6B **16**
Artisan Cres. *St Alb* —5E **15**
   (in two parts)

Art School Yd. St Alb —6F 15
   (off Chequer St.)
Arundel Gro. *St Alb* —2F **15**
Ashbourne Ct. *St Alb* —3C **20**
Ashby Gdns. *St Alb* —4F **19**
Ash Copse. *Brick W* —5B **22**
Ashcroft Clo. *Hpdn* —5G **5**
Ashdales. *St Alb* —4F **19**
Ash Gro. *Wheat* —4C **6**
Ashley Gdns. *Hpdn* —2H **3**
Ashley Rd. *St Alb* —6C **16**
Ashridge Dri. *Brick W* —4A **22**
Ashtree Ct. *St Alb* —6H **15**
Ashwell Pk. *Hpdn* —4F **5**
Ashwell St. *St Alb* —5F **15**
Ashwood M. *St Alb* —2F **19**
Aspasia Clo. *St Alb* —1H **19**
Aspen Clo. *Brick W* —4A **22**
Aubrey Av. *Lon C* —6C **20**
Aubrey La. *Redb* —5C **8**
Augustus Clo. *St Alb* —2C **18**
Avalon Clo. *Wat* —6A **22**
Avenue Rd. *St Alb* —5G **15**
Av. St Nicholas. *Hpdn* —4C **4**
Avon Ct. *Hpdn* —4D **4**
Avondale Ct. *St Alb* —6G **15**
Ayres End. —2H 11
Ayres End La. *Childw* —3E **11**
Ayres End La. *Hpdn* —6G **5**

Aysgarth Clo. *Hpdn* —5D **4**
Aysgarth Rd. *Redb* —1E **9**

Badingham Dri. *Hpdn* —5A **4**
Balfour Ct. *Hpdn* —2E **5**
(off Station Rd.)
Balmoral Clo. *Park* —2E **23**
Bardwell Ct. *St Alb* —1F **19**
(off Belmont Hill)
Bardwell Rd. *St Alb* —1F **19**
Barley Mow Cvn. Site. *St Alb*
—2F **21**
Barley Mow La. *St Alb* —3E **21**
Barley Ri. *Hpdn* —1E **5**
Barlings Rd. *Hpdn* —2D **10**
Barncroft Way. *St Alb* —1A **20**
Barnet Rd. *Lon C* —1E **25**
Barnfield Ct. *Hpdn* —5E **5**
Barnfield Rd. *Hpdn* —5E **5**
Barnfield Rd. *St Alb* —3C **16**
Barns Dene. *Hpdn* —3A **4**
Barons Row. *Hpdn* —6F **5**
Barry Clo. *St Alb* —5D **18**
Barton Clo. *Hpdn* —2E **5**
Barton Rd. *Wheat* —5C **6**
Bassett Clo. *Redb* —2F **9**
Batchwood Dri. *St Alb* —5D **14**
Batchwood Gdns. *St Alb* —5D **14**
Batchwood Hall. *St Alb* —3D **14**
Batchwood Vw. *St Alb* —4E **15**
Batford. —2F 5
Batford Mill Ind. Est. *Hpdn* —3F **5**
Batford Rd. *Hpdn* —2F **5**
Battlefield Rd. *St Alb* —4H **15**
Battleview. *Wheat* —5E **7**
Bay Tree Clo. *Park* —2E **23**
Beacon Ho. *St Alb* —6H **15**
Beaconsfield Rd. *St Alb* —6G **15**
Beaumonds Abbey Heights. *St Alb*
—6G **15**
Beaumont Av. *St Alb* —4B **16**
Beaumont Ct. *Hpdn* —4D **4**
Beaumont Hall La. *St Alb* —5F **9**
Beaumont Works. *St Alb* —6B **16**
Beckett's Av. *St Alb* —3E **15**
Bedford Pk. Rd. *St Alb* —6G **15**
Bedford Rd. *St Alb* —1G **19**
Bedmond La. *St Alb* —2B **18**
Beech Bottom. *St Alb* —3F **15**
Beech Clo. *Hpdn* —2E **11**
Beech Ct. *Hpdn* —2B **4**
Beech Cres. *Wheat* —6D **6**
Beeches, The. *Park* —1F **23**
Beech Farm Dri. *St Alb* —2F **17**
Beechfield Clo. *Redb* —2F **9**
Beech Hyde La. *Wheat* —6F **7**
Beeching Clo. *Hpdn* —1D **4**
Beech Pl. *St Alb* —3F **15**
Beech Rd. *St Alb* —3G **15**
Beechwood Av. *St Alb* —4B **16**
Beesonend Cotts. *Hpdn* —3D **10**
Beesonend La. *St Alb & Hpdn*
—5A **10**
Belgrave Clo. *St Alb* —2C **16**
Bellchambers Clo. *Lon C* —6C **20**
Bell La. *Lon C* —3E **25**
Bell Vw. *St Alb* —6D **16**
Belmont Ct. *St Alb* —1F **19**
Belmont Hill. *St Alb* —1F **19**
Belsize Clo. *St Alb* —1C **16**
Belvedere Gdns. *St Alb* —1C **22**
Ben Austins. *Redb* —3E **9**
Benbow Clo. *St Alb* —2B **20**
Bentsley Clo. *St Alb* —2C **16**
Beresford Rd. *St Alb* —1B **20**
Berkeley Ct. *Hpdn* —3C **4**
Berkeley Sq. *Hem H* —6A **8**
Berkley Clo. *St Alb* —2C **16**
Bernard's Heath. —3H 15
Bernard St. *St Alb* —5F **15**
Berners Dri. *St Alb* —3G **19**
Berries, The. *Sandr* —2A **16**
Betjeman Clo. *Hpdn* —4E **5**
Bettespol Meadows. *Redb* —1E **9**
Betty Entwistle Ho. *St Alb* —3F **19**
Beverley Gdns. *St Alb* —2D **16**
Bewdley Clo. *Hpdn* —1F **11**

Birch Copse. *Brick W* —4A **22**
Birchmead Clo. *St Alb* —3E **15**
Birch Way. *Hpdn* —5E **5**
Birch Way. *Lon C* —1D **24**
Birchwood Way. *Park* —2D **22**
Birklands La. *St Alb* —4B **20**
Birklands Pk. *St Alb* —4B **20**
Bishop's Clo. *St Alb* —2A **16**
Bishop's Gth. *St Alb* —2A **16**
Black Boy Wood. *Brick W* —4C **22**
Black Cut. *St Alb* —1G **19**
Blackhorse La. *Redb* —1E **9**
Black Lion Hill. *Shenl* —6E **25**
Blacksmiths La. *St Alb* —6D **14**
Blackthorn Clo. *St Alb* —3C **16**
Blake Clo. *St Alb* —3A **20**
Blandford Rd. *St Alb* —6A **16**
Blenheim Rd. *St Alb* —5H **15**
Blenkin Clo. *St Alb* —2E **15**
Bloomfield Rd. *Hpdn* —2B **4**
Blueberry Clo. *St Alb* —2F **15**
Bluebird Way. *Brick W* —4B **22**
Bluehouse Hill. *St Alb* —1C **18**
Bluett Rd. *Lon C* —1D **24**
Blundell Clo. *St Alb* —2F **15**
Blunts La. *St Alb* —5A **18**
Boissy Clo. *St Alb* —1E **21**
Boleyn Clo. *Hem H* —6A **8**
Boleyn Dri. *St Alb* —2F **19**
Bolingbrook. *St Alb* —2A **16**
Bond Ct. *Hpdn* —2B **4**
Boot All. St Alb —6F **15**
(off Chequer St.)
Borodale. *Hpdn* —4C **4**
Boswell Clo. *Shenl* —6E **25**
Boundary Rd. *St Alb* —4G **15**
Bower's Pde. *Hpdn* —4C **4**
Bowes Lyon M. *St Alb* —6F **15**
Bowgate. *St Alb* —5G **15**
Bowling Clo. *Hpdn* —6D **4**
Bowmans Open Farm. —6F 21
Bowyers Way. *Hpdn* —3C **4**
Brache Clo. *Redb* —2E **9**
Brackendale Gro. *Hpdn* —2H **3**
Brackendene. *Brick W* —4B **22**
Bramble Clo. *Hpdn* —2B **4**
Brambles, The. *St Alb* —2F **19**
Bramley Way. *St Alb* —1C **20**
Brampton Clo. *Hpdn* —4F **5**
Brampton Rd. *St Alb* —5A **16**
Branch Rd. *Park* —1F **23**
Branch Rd. *St Alb* —5D **14**
Brandon Mobile Home Pk. *St Alb*
—6D **16**
Breadcroft La. *Hpdn* —3D **4**
Breakspear Av. *St Alb* —1H **19**
Brecken Clo. *St Alb* —2A **16**
Brewhouse Hill. *Wheat* —5C **6**
Briar Rd. *St Alb* —3D **16**
Bricket Rd. *St Alb* —6F **15**
Bricket Wood. —4B 22
Brick Knoll Pk. *St Alb* —1C **20**
Bride Hall La. *Ay L* —2G **7**
Bridge Ct. *Hpdn* —2B **4**
Bridger Clo. *Wat* —6A **22**
Bridle Clo. *St Alb* —4G **15**
Brightview Clo. *Brick W* —3A **22**
Brinklow Ct. *St Alb* —3D **18**
Brinsmead. *Frog* —1F **23**
Britton Av. *St Alb* —6F **15**
Broad Acre. *Brick W* —4A **22**
Broad Colney. —3D 24
Broadfields. *Hpdn* —3B **4**
Broadlake Clo. *Lon C* —1D **24**
Broadley Gdns. *Shenl* —6E **25**
Broadstone Rd. *Hpdn* —1E **11**
Broadway, The. *St Alb* —6F **15**
Brocket Vw. *Wheat* —4D **6**
Brooke End. *Redb* —3E **9**
Brooklands Ct. St Alb —6G **15**
(off Hatfield Rd.)
Broom Corner. Hpdn —5E **5**
(off Broomfield Rd.)
Broomfield. *Park* —1E **23**
Broomleys. *St Alb* —3D **16**
Browning Rd. *Hpdn* —3E **5**
Bryant Ct. *Hpdn* —2C **4**
Bucknalls Clo. *Wat* —6A **22**

Bucknalls Dri. *Brick W* —5B **22**
Bucknalls La. *Wat* —6A **22**
Bull La. *Wheat* —1A **12**
Bull Rd. *Hpdn* —5D **4**
Bungalows, The. *Hpdn* —2E **5**
Burleigh Rd. *St Alb* —6B **16**
Burnham Rd. *St Alb* —6A **16**
Burnsall Pl. *Hpdn* —1E **11**
Burnside. *St Alb* —2B **20**
Burr Clo. *Lon C* —1E **25**
Burston Dri. *Park* —2E **23**
Burydell La. *Park* —1F **23**
Bury Grn. *Wheat* —5C **6**
Burywick. *Hpdn* —2D **10**
Butterfield La. *St Alb* —4G **19**
Butterfield Rd. *Wheat* —5C **6**
Buttermere Clo. *St Alb* —1B **20**
Butt Fld. Vw. *St Alb* —4E **19**
Buxton Clo. *St Alb* —3D **16**
Byron Pl. *Hem H* —6A **8**
Byron Rd. *Hpdn* —3C **4**

Caesars Rd. *Wheat* —5D **6**
Cairns Clo. *St Alb* —1D **20**
Caledon Rd. *Lon C* —6C **20**
Camberley Pl. *Hpdn* —1F **11**
Cambridge Rd. *St Alb* —1B **20**
Camlet Way. *St Alb* —5D **14**
Campfield Rd. *St Alb* —1A **20**
Camp Rd. *St Alb* —6H **15**
Camp, The. —1A 20
Camp Vw. Rd. *St Alb* —1B **20**
Canberra Clo. *St Alb* —2H **15**
Cannon St. *St Alb* —5F **15**
Canons Fld. *Wheat* —4D **6**
Cape Rd. *St Alb* —6B **16**
Cardinal Gro. *St Alb* —2D **18**
Carisbrooke Rd. *Hpdn* —3E **5**
Carisbrook Rd. *Park* —6D **18**
Carlbury Clo. *St Alb* —1B **20**
Carlisle Av. *St Alb* —4F **15**
Carlton Bank. *Hpdn* —4D **4**
Carlton Ct. *Hpdn* —4D **4**
Carlton Rd. *Hpdn* —3C **4**
Carnegie Rd. *St Alb* —2F **15**
Caroline Sharp Ho. *St Alb* —2C **16**
Carpenders Clo. *Hpdn* —1H **3**
Castle Ri. *Wheat* —3H **5**
Castle Rd. *St Alb* —6B **16**
Catham Clo. *St Alb* —2B **20**
Catherine Clo. *Hem H* —6A **8**
Catherine St. *St Alb* —5F **15**
Cavan Dri. *St Alb* —1F **15**
Cavan Rd. *Redb* —1E **9**
Cavendish Rd. *St Alb* —6H **15**
Caxton Cen. *Port W* —1H **15**
Cecil Rd. *St Alb* —6H **15**
Cedar Ct. *St Alb* —6D **16**
Cedars, The. *Hpdn* —4D **4**
Cedarwood Dri. *St Alb* —6D **16**
Cell Barnes Clo. *St Alb* —2B **20**
Cell Barnes La. *St Alb* —1A **20**
(in two parts)
Central Dri. *St Alb* —5C **16**
Century St. *St Alb* —5E **15**
Chad La. *Flam* —2A **2**
Chalfont Pl. *St Alb* —6G **15**
Chalkdell Fields. *St Alb* —3A **16**
Chamberlaines. *Hpdn* —1E **3**
Chancery Clo. *St Alb* —1D **16**
Chandlers Rd. *St Alb* —3C **16**
Chantry La. *Lon C* —6D **20**
Chapel Pl. *St Alb* —3F **19**
Chapel Rd. *Flam* —3A **2**
Charlotte Clo. *St Alb* —6E **17**
Charmouth Clo. *St Alb* —3A **16**
Charmouth Rd. *St Alb* —4A **16**
Charter Clo. *St Alb* —6F **15**
Charwood Clo. *Shenl* —6E **25**
Chatsworth Ct. *St Alb* —6H **15**
(off Granville Rd.)
Chaucer Wlk. *Hem H* —6A **8**
Cheltenham Ct. *St Alb* —1A **20**
(off Dexter Clo.)
Chene Dri. *St Alb* —4F **15**

Chenies, The. *Hpdn* —6E **5**
Chepstow. *Hpdn* —3B **4**
Chequer La. *Redb* —3E **9**
Chequers Hill. *Mark* —3A **2**
Chequer St. *St Alb* —6F **15**
Cheriton Clo. *St Alb* —6F **15**
Cherry Hill. *St Alb* —5C **18**
Cherry Tree Av. *Lon C* —6D **20**
Cherry Tree La. *Wheat* —4A **6**
Chesterton Av. *Hpdn* —4E **5**
Chestnut Dri. *St Alb* —4B **16**
Chicken La. *Lon C* —1D **24**
Childwick Green. —5E 11
Chiltern Ct. *Hpdn* —4E **5**
Chiltern Ct. St Alb —2D **16**
(off Twyford Rd.)
Chiltern Rd. *St Alb* —1C **16**
Chime Sq. *St Alb* —5G **15**
Chiswell Green. —5A 18
Chiswellgreen La. *St Alb* —5A **18**
Chivenor Pl. *St Alb* —2C **20**
Chowns, The. *Hpdn* —2C **10**
Christchurch Clo. *St Alb* —5F **15**
Christopher Pl. St Alb —6F **15**
(off Verulam Rd.)
Church Cres. *St Alb* —5E **15**
Church Cft. *St Alb* —2C **20**
Church End. —3E 9
Church End. *Flam* —4A **2**
Church End. *Redb* —3E **9**
Church End. *Sandr* —5C **12**
Churchfield. *St Alb* —5E **5**
Church Grn. *Hpdn* —4C **4**
Church Grn. Row. *Hpdn* —4C **4**
Churchill Rd. *St Alb* —5A **16**
Church La. *Col H* —2H **21**
Church La. *Flam* —3A **2**
Church St. *St Alb* —5F **15**
Church St. *Wheat* —5D **6**
Civic Clo. *St Alb* —6F **15**
Clare Ct. *St Alb* —1H **19**
Claremont. *Brick W* —5C **22**
Clarence Rd. *Hpdn* —2C **4**
Clarence Rd. *St Alb* —6H **15**
Clarendon Rd. *Hpdn* —2C **4**
Claudian Pl. *St Alb* —1C **18**
Claygate Av. *Hpdn* —3A **4**
Cleave, The. *Hpdn* —4F **5**
Clifton St. *St Alb* —5G **15**
Cloister Gth. *St Alb* —4G **19**
Close, The. *Hpdn* —1G **3**
Close, The. *Rad* —6H **23**
Close, The. *St Alb* —3E **19**
Coach La. *Hpdn* —5C **4**
Coates Way. *Wat* —6A **22**
Cockle Way. *Shenl* —6E **25**
Codicote Rd. *Wheat & Welw*
—4D **6**
Cold Harbour. —1E 5
Coldharbour La. *Hpdn* —1D **4**
Coleman Green. —2F 13
Coleman Grn. La. *Wheat* —4C **12**
Coleridge Ct. *Hpdn* —4D **4**
Coleridge Cres. *Hem H* —6A **8**
Coles La. *Pep* —1C **2**
Coleswood Rd. *Hpdn* —6E **5**
Colindale Av. *St Alb* —2H **19**
College Clo. *Flam* —4A **2**
College Pl. *St Alb* —6E **15**
College Rd. *St Alb* —1B **20**
College St. *St Alb* —6F **15**
Collens Rd. *Hpdn* —2D **10**
Collingwood Dri. *Lon C* —5D **20**
Collyer Rd. *Lon C* —1D **24**
Colnbrook Clo. *Lon C* —1E **25**
Colne Gdns. *Lon C* —1E **25**
Colney Heath. —2H 21
Colney Heath La. *St Alb* —1E **21**
Colney Street. —4H 23
Common La. *Hpdn* —1F **5**
Common, The. *Hpdn* —1F **3**
Common, The. *Redb* —2F **9**
Compton Gdns. *St Alb* —6D **18**
Coningsby Bank. *St Alb* —4F **19**
Connaught Rd. *Hpdn* —3D **4**
Connaught Rd. *St Alb* —4E **15**
Conquerors Hill. *Wheat* —5E **7**
Coombes Rd. *Lon C* —6C **20**

Coopers Green—Hammers Ga.

Coopers Green. —1H 17
Coopers Grn. La. St Alb —3E 17
Coopers Mdw. Redb —1E 9
Coopers M. Hpdn —5C 4
Cooters End La. Hpdn & E Hyde
—1A 4
Copper Beeches. Hpdn —4D 4
Copse, The. Wat —6A 22
Corby Clo. St Alb —5C 18
Corder Clo. St Alb —3C 18
Corinium Ga. St Alb —2C 18
Cornwall Rd. Hpdn —3D 4
Cornwall Rd. St Alb —2G 19
Corringham Ct. St Alb —5H 15
Cory-Wright Way. Wheat —4E 7
Cosne M. Hpdn —6E 5
Cotlandswick. Lon C —5C 20
Cotsmoor. St Alb —6H 15
(off Granville Rd.)
Cotswold Clo. St Alb —1C 16
Cottonmill Cres. St Alb —1F 19
Cottonmill La. St Alb —2F 19
Coursers Rd. Col H —1G 25
Courtfields. Hpdn —4F 5
Courtyard, The. St Alb —6F 17
Cowper Rd. Hpdn —4D 4
Cox Clo. Shenl —6F 25
Crabtree La. Hpdn —5D 4
(in two parts)
Craiglands. St Alb —2D 16
Cranbourne Dri. Hpdn —1E 11
Cranbrook Dri. St Alb —6E 17
Cranefield Dri. Wat —6A 22
Cranford Ct. Hpdn —4E 5
Cranmore Ct. St Alb —5H 15
(off Avenue Rd.)
Cranwell St Alb —2C 20
Cravells Rd. Hpdn —1D 10
Crecy Gdns. Redb —1E 9
Creighton Av. St Alb —4F 19
Crescent, The. Brick W —4C 22
Cricketers Clo. St Alb —5G 15
Croft Ct. Hpdn —4D 4
(off Breadcroft La.)
Croft, The. St Alb —5C 18
Croftwell. Hpdn —5H 5
Cromer Hyde. —2H 13
Cromer Hyde La. Wheat & Lem
—1H 13
Cromwell Clo. St Alb —1D 16
Crosby Clo. St Alb —3C 20
Crossfields. St Alb —3D 18
Cross La. Hpdn —2D 10
Crosspaths. Hpdn —1G 3
Cross St. St Alb —6F 15
Cross Way. Hpdn —2E 5
Crosthwaite Ct. Hpdn —3D 4
Crouch Hall Gdns. Redb —1E 9
Crouch Hall La. Redb —1E 9
Crown St. Redb —2F 9
Cuckmans Dri. St Alb —5C 18
Cuffley Ct. Hem H —6A 8
Culver Rd. St Alb —5G 15
Cumberland Ct. St Alb —5F 15
Cumberland Dri. Redb —1F 9
Cunningham Av. St Alb —2H 19
Cunningham Hill Rd. St Alb
—2H 19
Cutmore Dri. Col H —2H 21
Cyrils Way. St Alb —3F 19

Dalewood. Hpdn —4F 5
Dalkeith Rd. Hpdn —3E 5
Dalton St. St Alb —5F 15
Damson Way. St Alb —4C 16
Dane Clo. Hpdn —1E 5
Danes, The. Park —2E 23
Darblay Clo. Sandr —2F 13
Dark La. Hpdn —6F 5
Darley Cft. Park —2D 22
Darwin Clo. Hem H —6A 8
Darwin Clo. St Alb —2G 15
Davis Ct. St Alb —6G 15
Davys Clo. Wheat —6E 7
Deacon Clo. St Alb —4F 19
Dean Moore Clo. St Alb —1E 19
Dean's Gdns. St Alb —2A 16

Deerings, The. Hpdn —2C 10
De Havilland Ct. Shenl —6E 25
Dell Clo. Hpdn —2D 4
Dellcroft Way. Hpdn —1C 10
Dellfield. St Alb —1H 19
Dell Ri. Park —6D 18
Dell, The. St Alb —4A 16
Delmerend La. Flam —3A 2
Derwent Rd. Hpdn —1G 3
De Tany Ct. St Alb —1F 19
Deva Clo. St Alb —2C 18
Devon Ct. St Alb —1G 19
Devonshire Rd. Hpdn —3D 4
Dexter Clo. St Alb —1A 20
Dickens Clo. St Alb —5F 15
Doggetts Way. St Alb —2E 19
Dolphin Yd. St Alb —1F 19
(off Holywell Hill)
Dorant Ho. St Alb —2F 15
Dorchester Ct. St Alb —1A 20
(off Dexter Clo.)
Dormie Clo. St Alb —4E 15
Douglas Rd. Hpdn —3B 4
Down Edge. Redb —2D 8
Downedge. St Alb —5D 14
Downes Rd. St Alb —2B 16
Down Grn. La. Wheat —5B 6
Drakes Dri. St Alb —3B 20
Driftwood Av. St Alb —6C 18
Drive, The. Hpdn —4C 4
Drive, The. Naps —5A 20
Drop La. Brick W —4D 22
Drovers La. Wheat —2D 12
Drovers Way. St Alb —6F 15
Dubrae Clo. St Alb —2C 18
Duncan Ct. St Alb —2H 19
Dunstable Rd. Flam —3C 2
Dunstable Rd. Redb —6E 3
Dyke La. Wheat —1D 12
Dymoke Grn. St Alb —2A 16

Eastbury Ct. St Alb —5H 15
East Clo. St Alb —5D 18
East Comn. Redb —3E 9
Eastcote Dri. Hpdn —1F 11
East Dri. Naps —1A 24
East Dri. Oakl —5E 17
Eastfield Ct. St Alb —3D 16
East La. Wheat —4D 6
Eastmoor Ct. Hpdn —1E 11
Eastmoor Pk. Hpdn —6E 5
East Mt. Wheat —4D 6
Eaton Rd. St Alb —6B 16
Edgbaston Dri. Shenl —6E 25
Edison Clo. St Alb —1C 20
Edmund Beaufort Dri. St Alb
—4F 15
Edward Clo. St Alb —1H 19
Eleanor Av. St Alb —4F 15
Elizabeth Ct. St Alb —3D 16
(in two parts)
Elliswick Rd. Hpdn —3D 4
Elm Dri. St Alb —6C 16
Ely Rd. St Alb —1B 20
Englehurst. Hpdn —4F 5
Enid Clo. Brick W —5B 22
Ennerdale Clo. St Alb —2B 20
Ennis Clo. Hpdn —1F 11
Eric Steele Ho. Park —1D 22
Ermine Clo. St Alb —1C 18
Eskdale. Lon C —1F 25
Essex St. St Alb —5G 15
Etna Rd. St Alb —5F 15
Evans Gro. St Alb —2C 16
Everard Clo. St Alb —2F 19
Everlasting La. St Alb —5E 15
(in two parts)
Executive Pk. St Alb —6B 16
Eywood Rd. St Alb —2E 19

Faircross Way. St Alb —4A 16
Fairfield Clo. Hpdn —4F 5
Fairhaven. Park —1F 23
Fairmead Av. Hpdn —5E 5
Fairway Clo. Hpdn —2C 10
Fairway Clo. Park —1E 23

Falconers Fld. Hpdn —2H 3
Fallows Grn. Hpdn —2D 4
Falmouth Ct. St Alb —4E 15
Farm Av. Hpdn —1H 3
Farm Clo. Hpdn —1H 3
Farm Clo. Shenl —4E 25
Farm Rd. St Alb —5B 16
Farriday Clo. St Alb —2G 15
Farringford Clo. St Alb —6C 18
Faulkner Ct. St Alb —4G 15
(off Boundary Rd.)
Ferndene. Brick W —5B 22
Fernecroft. St Alb —3F 19
Fernleys. St Alb —3C 16
Ferrers La. Hpdn —2H 11
Field Clo. Hpdn —6F 5
Field Clo. Sandr —2A 16
Fielders Way. Shenl —6E 25
Fieldfares. Lon C —1D 24
Field Ho. Ct. Hpdn —3C 4
Field Vw. Ri. Brick W —3A 22
Finley Rd. Hpdn —2F 5
Firbank Rd. St Alb —2H 15
Firs, The. Hpdn —3F 5
Firs, The. St Alb —4B 20
Firwood Av. St Alb —6E 17
Fishpool St. St Alb —6D 14
Fish St. Redb —2F 9
Fish St. Farm. Redb —2F 9
Five Acres. Lon C —5D 20
Five Acres Av. Brick W —3B 22
Flamstead. —3A 2
Flamsteadbury. Redb —2C 8
Flamsteadbury La. Redb —3E 9
Flavian Clo. St Alb —2B 18
Fleetville. —6B 16
Flinders Clo. St Alb —2A 20
Flint Copse. Redb —1G 9
Flint Way. St Alb —2E 15
Flora Gro. St Alb —1H 19
Floral Dri. Lon C —6D 20
Florence Ct. St Alb —1G 19
Flowton Gro. Hpdn —6C 4
Folly Av. St Alb —5E 15
Folly Fields. Wheat —3B 6
Folly La. St Alb —5E 15
Folly, The. —3B 6
Fontmell Clo. St Alb —3G 15
Forefield. St Alb —1C 22
Forge End. St Alb —6C 18
Four Limes. Wheat —5D 6
Four Trees. St Alb —5D 18
Fovant Clo. Hpdn —1E 11
Foxcroft. St Alb —2A 20
Francis Av. St Alb —3F 15
French Row. St Alb —6F 15
Friar's Wash. —2A 2
Frobisher Rd. St Alb —2C 20
Frogmore. —2G 23
Frogmore. Park & St Alb —1F 23
Frogmore Home Pk. Frog —1F 23
Fryth Mead. St Alb —5D 14
Fulmore Clo. Hpdn —1F 5
Furse Av. St Alb —3A 16
Furzebushes La. St Alb —5A 18
Furzedown Ct. Hpdn —5D 4

Gaddesden La. Hem H & Redb
—3A 8
Gainsborough Av. St Alb —5H 15
Garden Clo. Hpdn —2C 10
Garden Clo. St Alb —5B 16
Garden Cotts. Frog —1F 23
Garden Ct. Wheat —4D 6
Gardens of the Rose. —6B 18
Garnett Dri. Brick W —3B 22
Garrard Way. Wheat —5D 6
Gatcombe Ct. St Alb —1A 20
(off Dexter Clo.)
George St. St Alb —6F 15
Gerard Ct. Hpdn —3C 4
Gertrude Peake Pl. Redb —2F 9
(off High St.)
Gibbons Clo. Sandr —6C 12
Gibraltar Lodge. Hpdn —2F 5
Gidian Ct. Park —1F 23

Gilbert Ct. Hpdn —1D 4
Giles Clo. Sandr —6C 12
Gillian Av. St Alb —4E 19
Gilpin Grn. Hpdn —4E 5
Gladeside. St Alb —3D 16
Gleave Clo. St Alb —5B 16
Glemsford Dri. Hpdn —3F 5
Glenbower Clo. St Alb —6D 16
Glenferrie Rd. St Alb —6A 16
Glengall Pl. St Alb —3G 19
Glenlyn Av. St Alb —1B 20
Glevum Clo. St Alb —2B 18
Globe Clo. Hpdn —4D 4
Goldsmith Way. St Alb —5E 15
Gombards. St Alb —5F 15
Gordon Clo. St Alb —1B 20
Gordon Ho. St Alb —1B 20
Gordons Wlk. Hpdn —5E 5
Gorham Dri. St Alb —3G 19
Gorse Corner. Hpdn —5E 5
(off Barnfield Rd.)
Gorse Corner. St Alb —4F 15
Gorselands. Hpdn —6E 5
Grafton Clo. St Alb —1D 20
Graham Clo. St Alb —2F 19
Granary Clo. Wheat —5D 6
Granary La. Hpdn —4D 4
Granby Av. Hpdn —3E 5
Grange Ct. St Alb —5F 15
Grange Ct. Rd. Hpdn —1E 11
Grange St. St Alb —5F 15
Grant Gdns. Hpdn —3D 4
Granville Ct. St Alb —6H 15
(off Granville Rd.)
Granville Rd. St Alb —6H 15
Grasmere Av. Hpdn —3E 5
Grasmere Rd. St Alb —2B 20
Grassington Clo. Brick W —4C 22
Greatfield Clo. Hpdn —1G 3
Greenbanks. St Alb —2H 19
Green La. Hpdn —6F 5
Green La. Lon C —4A 20
Green La. St Alb —3E 15
Green La. Clo. Hpdn —5G 5
Greensleeves Clo. St Alb —1C 20
Green, The. Lon C —1D 24
Greenway. Hpdn —5F 5
Greenwich Ct. St Alb —1A 20
Greenwood Gdns. Shenl —6E 25
Grenadier Clo. St Alb —1C 20
Gresford Clo. St Alb —6D 16
Greyfriars La. Hpdn —6C 4
Griffiths Way. St Alb —2E 19
Grimsdyke Lodge. St Alb —6A 16
Grimston Rd. St Alb —1H 19
Grimthorpe Clo. St Alb —3F 15
Grindcobbe. St Alb —3F 19
Groom Ct. St Alb —5A 16
Grosvenor Rd. St Alb —1G 19
Grove Av. Hpdn —6F 5
Grovebury Gdns. Park —1E 23
Grovelands. Park —1D 22
Grove Rd. Hpdn —6E 5
Grove Rd. St Alb —1F 19
Gryphon Ind. Pk., The. Port W
—2H 15
Guildford Rd. St Alb —1B 20
Gurney Ct. Rd. St Alb —4H 15
Gustard Wood. —1C 6

Haddon Ct. Hpdn —4D 4
Hadleigh Ct. Hpdn —6G 5
Hadrian Clo. St Alb —2B 18
Haig Clo. St Alb —1B 20
Haig Ho. St Alb —1B 20
Hales Mdw. Hpdn —3C 4
Half Moon M. St Alb —6F 15
Hall Heath Clo. St Alb —4B 16
Halliday Clo. Shenl —6E 25
Hall Pl. Clo. St Alb —5G 15
Hall Pl. Gdns. St Alb —5G 15
Halsey Pk. Lon C —2F 25
Halton Clo. Park —2E 23
Hamilton Clo. Brick W —5C 22
Hamilton Rd. St Alb —5A 16
Hamlet Clo. Brick W —4B 22
Hammers Ga. St Alb —6C 18

Manor Rd.—Redding La.

Manor Rd. *Wheat* —3G **5**
Mansdale Rd. *Redb* —3D **8**
Manston Way. *St Alb* —1D **20**
Maple Av. *St Alb* —2E **15**
Maple Cotts. *Hpdn* —2D **10**
Maplefield. *Park* —3D **22**
Maple Rd. *Hpdn* —4B **4**
Maples. *Hpdn* —2C **4**
Marconi Way. *St Alb* —6D **16**
Marford Rd. *Wheat & Lem* —5D **6**
Margaret Av. *St Alb* —4F **15**
Market Pl. *St Alb* —6F **15**
Marlborough Bldgs. *St Alb* —6G **15**
Marlborough Ga. *St Alb* —6G **15**
Marlborough Rd. *St Alb* —6G **15**
Marquis Clo. *Hpdn* —3F **5**
Marquis La. *Hpdn* —3F **5**
Marshall Av. *St Alb* —3G **15**
Marshalls Heath. —3A 6
Marshalls Heath La. *Wheat* —3A **6**
Marshalls Way. *Wheat* —3H **5**
Marshal's Dri. *St Alb* —3A **16**
Marshalswick. —3B 16
Marshalswick La. *St Alb* —3A **16**
Marten Ga. *St Alb* —2A **16**
Martham Ct. *Hpdn* —2E **5**
Martins Ct. *St Alb* —3C **20**
Martyr Clo. *St Alb* —4F **19**
Masefield Ct. *Hpdn* —1D **4**
Masefield Rd. *Hpdn* —2D **4**
Maslen Rd. *St Alb* —3C **20**
Maxwell Rd. *St Alb* —1B **20**
May Clo. *St Alb* —4F **15**
Mayfair Clo. *St Alb* —1C **16**
Mayfield Clo. *Hpdn* —2A **4**
Mayflower Rd. *Park* —1D **22**
Maynard Dri. *St Alb* —3F **19**
Mayne Av. *St Alb* —2B **18**
Meadow Clo. *Brick W* —3C **22**
Meadow Clo. *Lon C* —1D **24**
Meadow Clo. *St Alb* —3C **16**
Meadowcroft. *St Alb* —3A **20**
Meadow Wlk. *Hpdn* —5E **5**
Meads La. *Wheat* —4D **6**
Meads, The. *Brick W* —3B **22**
Meadway. *Hpdn* —6G **5**
Meautys. *St Alb* —2B **18**
Medlows. *Hpdn* —3A **4**
Melbourne Clo. *St Alb* —2C **16**
Mendip Clo. *St Alb* —2C **16**
Mentmore Rd. *St Alb* —2F **19**
Mercers Row. *St Alb* —4A **16**
Mereden Ct. St Alb —3E 19
  (off Tavistock Av.)
Merlin Cen., The. *St Alb* —6F **17**
Merryfields. *St Alb* —6E **17**
Metro Cen. *St Alb* —2H **15**
Mews, The. *Hpdn* —4D **4**
Middlefield Clo. *St Alb* —3C **16**
Midway. *St Alb* —3D **18**
Mile Ho. Clo. *St Alb* —3A **20**
Mile Ho. La. *St Alb* —4H **19**
Milford Clo. *St Alb* —2D **16**
Milford Hill. *Hpdn* —1F **5**
Millers Ri. *St Alb* —1G **19**
Milliner's Ct. *St Alb* —6G **15**
Mill Vw. *Park* —1F **23**
Mill Wlk. Wheat —4D 6
  (off High St.)
Milton Ct. *Hpdn* —4D **4**
Milton Ct. *Hem H* —6A **8**
Milton Dene. *Hem H* —6A **8**
Milton Rd. *Hpdn* —4D **4**
Minister Ct. *Frog* —2G **23**
Mitchell Clo. *St Alb* —4F **19**
Molescroft Ridge Av. *Hpdn* —1H **3**
Monastery Clo. *St Alb* —6E **15**
Monks Clo. *Redb* —2F **9**
Monks Clo. *St Alb* —2G **19**
Monks Horton Way. *St Alb*
  —4A **16**
Mons Clo. *Hpdn* —1F **11**
Moorland Rd. *Hpdn* —1D **4**
Moorlands. *Frog* —2G **23**
Moor Mill La. *Col S* —3G **23**
  (in two parts)
Moran Clo. *Brick W* —5B **22**
Moreton Av. *Hpdn* —3B **4**

Moreton End Clo. *Hpdn* —3B **4**
Moreton End La. *Hpdn* —3B **4**
Moreton Pl. *Hpdn* —2B **4**
Morris Way. *Lon C* —6D **20**
Mosquito Aircraft Mus. —3G 25
Moss Side. *Brick W* —4B **22**
Mountbatten Clo. *St Alb* —3B **20**
Mount Dri. *Park* —5F **19**
Mt. Pleasant. *St Alb* —5D **14**
Mt. Pleasant La. *Brick W* —4A **22**
Mount Rd. *Wheat* —4D **6**
Mount Vw. *Lon C* —1E **25**
Mud La. *Hpdn* —2F **11**
Mulberry Clo. *Park* —2D **22**
Murton Ct. *St Alb* —5G **15**
Myers Clo. *Shenl* —6E **25**

Nairn Clo. *Hpdn* —1F **11**
Napier Clo. *Lon C* —5D **20**
Napsbury. —1C 24
Napsbury Av. *Lon C* —6C **20**
Napsbury La. *St Alb* —3A **20**
Necton Rd. *Wheat* —5E **7**
Nell Gwynn Clo. *Shenl* —6E **25**
Nelson Av. *St Alb* —3B **20**
Netherfield Rd. *Hpdn* —3D **10**
Netherway. *St Alb* —3C **18**
New England St. *St Alb* —6E **15**
Newfield Way. *St Alb* —2C **20**
New Forge Pl. *Redb* —2F **9**
Newgate Clo. *St Alb* —3D **16**
New Greens. —2F 15
New Greens Av. *St Alb* —1F **15**
New Ho. Pk. *St Alb* —3A **20**
New Kent Rd. *St Alb* —6F **15**
Newland Clo. *St Alb* —3A **20**
Newlyn Clo. *Brick W* —4A **22**
Newmans Dri. *Hpdn* —3B **4**
Newmarket Ct. *St Alb* —5E **15**
Newton Clo. *Hpdn* —1F **11**
Nicholas Clo. *St Alb* —3F **15**
Nicholas Ho. *St Alb* —1D **20**
Nicholls Clo. *Redb* —2D **8**
Nightingale La. *St Alb* —3C **20**
  (in two parts)
Nightingale Wlk. *Hem H* —6A **8**
Nimrod Clo. *St Alb* —4C **16**
Ninnings Cotts. *Hpdn* —5C **4**
Noke La. *St Alb* —6A **18**
Noke Shot. *Hpdn* —1E **5**
Noke Side. *St Alb* —1C **22**
Nomansland. —1D 12
Normandy Rd. *St Alb* —4F **15**
North Av. *Shenl* —6E **25**
Northaw Clo. *Hem H* —6A **8**
N. Barnes Av. *St Alb* —3A **20**
North Clo. *St Alb* —5D **18**
North Comn. *Redb* —3E **9**
  (in two parts)
North Cotts. *Naps* —5A **20**
North Dri. *Oakl* —4E **17**
Northfield Rd. *Hpdn* —1E **5**
N. Orbital Rd. *Lon C & Col H*
  —4C **20**
N. Orbital Rd. *St Alb & Lon C*
  —4F **19**
N. Orbital Rd. *Wat & Brick W*
  —6A **22**
N. Orbital Trad. Est. *St Alb* —4A **20**
North Riding. *Brick W* —4C **22**
Northside. *Sandr* —6B **12**
Nunnery Clo. *St Alb* —2G **19**
Nunnery Stables. *St Alb* —2F **19**
Nuns La. *St Alb* —4G **19**
Nurseries Rd. *Wheat* —6E **7**

Oak Av. *Brick W* —4C **22**
Oakdene Way. *St Alb* —6C **16**
Oakfield Rd. *Hpdn* —2B **10**
Oakhurst Av. *Hpdn* —1B **10**
Oaklands La. *Smal* —4E **17**
Oakley Rd. *Hpdn* —6F **5**
Oakridge. *Brick W* —3B **22**
Oakridge La. *A'ham & Rad* —6H **23**
Oakview Clo. *Hpdn* —2B **10**
Oak Way. *Hpdn* —2C **10**

Oakwood Dri. *Hpdn* —2B **10**
Oakwood Dri. *St Alb* —5C **16**
Oakwood Rd. *Brick W* —3B **22**
Offa Rd. *St Alb* —6E **15**
Offas Way. *Wheat* —5D **6**
Old Brewhouse, The. *Wheat*
  —5C **6**
Old Cotts. *St Alb* —3E **25**
Oldfield Ct. *St Alb* —1G **19**
Oldfield Rd. *Lon C* —5D **20**
Old Garden Ct. *St Alb* —6E **15**
Old Harpenden Rd. *St Alb* —2G **15**
Old London Rd. *St Alb* —1F **19**
Old Oak. *St Alb* —3G **19**
Old Orchard. *Park* —6E **19**
Old Parkbury La. *Col S* —3H **23**
Old Rectory Clo. *Hpdn* —3C **4**
Old Rectory Gdns. *Wheat* —4D **6**
Old Sopwell Gdns. *St Alb* —2G **19**
Old Station Bus. Cen., The. *St Alb*
  —2H **19**
Old Watford Rd. *Brick W* —4A **22**
Oliver Clo. *Park* —1F **23**
Orchard Av. *Hpdn* —4B **4**
Orchard Clo. *St Alb* —1H **19**
Orchard Dri. *Park* —1D **22**
Orchard Ho. La. *St Alb* —1F **19**
Orchard St. *St Alb* —1E **19**
Orient Clo. *St Alb* —2G **19**
Orton Clo. *St Alb* —2B **16**
Oster St. *St Alb* —5E **15**
Oswald Rd. *St Alb* —1G **19**
Otterton Clo. *Hpdn* —2B **4**
Oulton Ri. *Hpdn* —2E **5**
Overstone Rd. *Hpdn* —4E **5**
Overtrees. *Hpdn* —2B **4**
Oxford Av. *St Alb* —1C **20**
Ox La. *Hpdn* —2D **4**
Oysterfields. *St Alb* —5D **14**

Packhorse Clo. *St Alb* —3C **16**
Paddock End. *Hpdn* —6G **5**
Paddock Wood. *Hpdn* —6G **5**
Pageant Rd. *St Alb* —1F **19**
Palfrey Clo. *St Alb* —4F **15**
Park Av. *St Alb* —5A **16**
Park Av. N. *Hpdn* —4A **4**
Park Av. S. *Hpdn* —4A **4**
Park Corner. —3H 21
Park Hill. *Hpdn* —3B **4**
Park Homes. *Lon C* —6C **20**
Parkinson Clo. *Wheat* —5D **6**
Parklands Dri. *St Alb* —1C **18**
Park La. *Col H* —3H **21**
Park Mt. *Hpdn* —3B **4**
Park Pl. *Park* —1F **23**
Park Ri. *Hpdn* —2A **4**
Park Ri. Clo. *Hpdn* —2A **4**
Park Street. —6F 19
Park St. *Park* —6F **19**
Park St. La. *Brick W & Park*
  —4D **22**
Park, The. *Redb* —3F **9**
Park, The. *St Alb* —4A **16**
Pk. View Clo. *St Alb* —1A **20**
Parkway Ct. *St Alb* —3D **20**
Parr Cres. *Hem H* —6A **8**
Parson's Clo. *Flam* —4A **2**
Partridge Rd. *St Alb* —2F **15**
Parva Clo. *Hpdn* —1F **11**
Pastures, The. *St Alb* —4C **18**
Pat Larner Ho. St Alb —1F 19
  (off Belmont Hill)
Paxton Rd. *St Alb* —1G **19**
Peakes Pl. St Alb —6H 15
  (off Granville Rd.)
Pearces Wlk. St Alb —1F 19
  (off Albert St.)
Pemberton Clo. *St Alb* —3F **19**
Pendennis Ct. *Hpdn* —6F **5**
Penman Clo. *St Alb* —1C **22**
Penn Rd. *Park* —1E **23**
Penny Cft. *Hpdn* —3C **10**
Penshurst Clo. *Hpdn* —1H **3**
Peppard Clo. *Redb* —2D **8**
Perham Way. *Lon C* —6D **20**
Permain Clo. *Shenl* —6E **25**

Peters Av. *Lon C* —6C **20**
Petersfield. *St Alb* —2G **15**
Pickford Hill. *Hpdn* —2E **5**
Pickford Rd. *St Alb* —6B **16**
Pie Corner. *Flam* —3A **2**
Pie Garden. *Flam* —4A **2**
Pigeonwick. *Hpdn* —2D **4**
Piggottshill La. *Hpdn* —6E **5**
Pilgrim Clo. *Park* —1E **23**
Pilgrims Clo. *Wat* —6A **22**
Pine Gro. *Brick W* —4B **22**
Pine Ridge. *St Alb* —3A **20**
Pinewood Clo. *St Alb* —6C **16**
Pipers Av. *Hpdn* —6F **5**
Pipers Clo. *Redb* —1E **9**
Pipers La. *Hpdn* —6G **5**
Pippin Clo. *Shenl* —6E **25**
Pirton Clo. *St Alb* —1C **16**
Pitstone Clo. *St Alb* —1C **16**
Pitt Dri. *St Alb* —3C **20**
Place Farm. *Wheat* —4D **6**
Pleasance, The. *Hpdn* —1H **3**
Poets Ct. *Hpdn* —4D **4**
Pollicott Clo. *St Alb* —1C **16**
Pondfield Cres. *St Alb* —2B **16**
Pondsmeade. *Redb* —2F **9**
Pondwick Rd. *Hpdn* —3A **4**
Pondwicks Clo. *St Alb* —1E **19**
Poplars, The. *St Alb* —4B **20**
Porters Hill. *Hpdn* —1E **5**
Porters Pk. Dri. *Shenl* —6E **25**
Porters Wood. *St Alb* —2H **15**
Portland St. *St Alb* —6E **15**
Portman Clo. *St Alb* —1C **16**
Portman Ho. *St Alb* —3F **15**
Potters Crouch. —4A 18
Potterscrouch La. *St Alb* —4A **18**
Potters Fld. *St Alb* —2G **15**
Poultney Clo. *Shenl* —6F **25**
Pound Clo. *Sandr* —5C **12**
Poynings Clo. *Hpdn* —5H **5**
Prae Clo. *St Alb* —5D **14**
Praetorian Ct. *St Alb* —3E **19**
Princess Diana Dri. *St Alb* —1D **20**
Priory Ct. *St Alb* —1G **19**
Priory Orchard. *Flam* —3A **2**
Priory, The. Redb —2F 9
  (off High St.)
Priory Wlk. *St Alb* —3G **19**
Prospect La. *Hpdn* —3B **10**
Prospect Rd. *St Alb* —2F **19**
Pudding La. St Alb —6F 15
  (off Chequer St.)
Puddingstone Dri. *St Alb* —2C **20**
Pullman Clo. *St Alb* —2G **19**
Punch Bowl La. *Hem H* —6G **9**
Putterills, The. *Hpdn* —3C **4**

Quadrant, The. *St Alb* —3B **16**
Quantock Clo. *St Alb* —2C **16**
Queens Ct. *St Alb* —6B **16**
Queens Cres. *St Alb* —3B **16**
Queen's Rd. *Hpdn* —6D **4**
Queen St. *St Alb* —6E **15**
Queens Way. *Shenl* —6E **25**

Radlett Rd. *Frog & Col S* —3G **23**
Ragged Hall La. *St Alb* —4A **18**
Rainbow Clo. *Redb* —1D **8**
Ramparts, The. *St Alb* —1D **18**
Ramsbury Rd. *St Alb* —1G **19**
Ramsey Clo. *St Alb* —2A **20**
Ramsey Lodge Ct. *St Alb* —5G **15**
Randalls Wlk. *Brick W* —4B **22**
Ranleigh Wlk. *Hpdn* —1F **11**
Raphael Clo. *Shenl* —6E **25**
Ravenscroft. *Hpdn* —1F **11**
Raymer Clo. *St Alb* —5G **15**
Rectory La. *Shenl* —6G **25**
Redbourn. —2F 9
Redbournbury La. *St Alb* —5H **9**
Redbourn Ind. Est. *Redb* —2F **9**
Redbourn La. *Redb* —1G **9**
Redbourn Rd. *Hem H* —6A **8**
Redbourn Rd. *St Alb* —5G **9**
Redding La. *Redb* —4C **2**